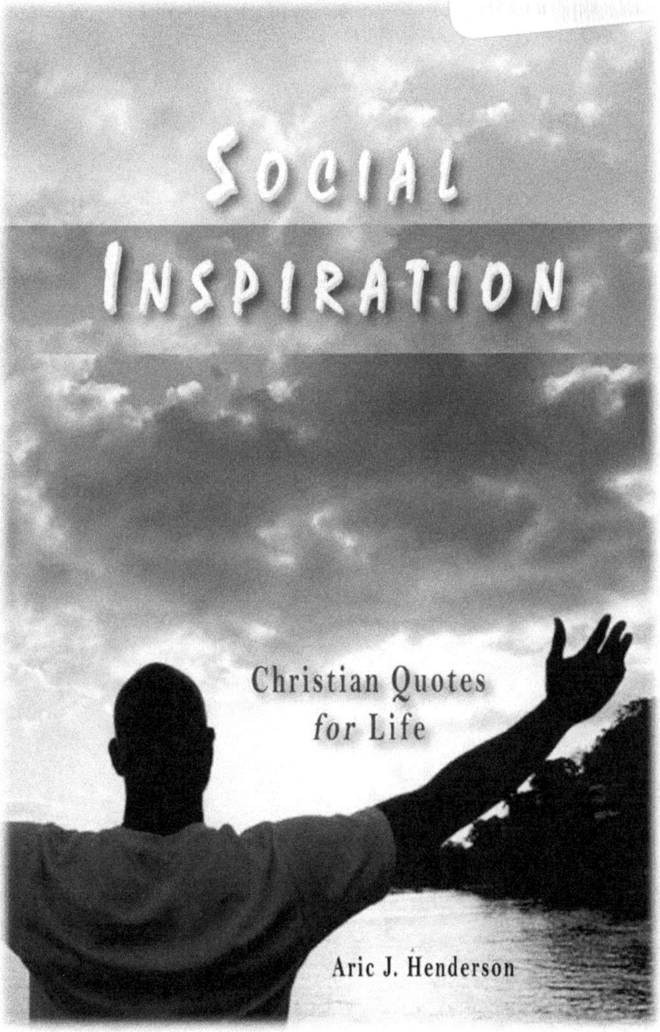

Social Inspiration

Christian Quotes for Life

Aric J. Henderson

Raymore, MO 64083

Social Inspiration   Aric J. Henderson

SOCIAL INSPIRATION
Copyright ©2010. Aric J. Henderson
Published by Inspirations by Grace LaJoy
Raymore, MO 64083
www.gracelajoy.com

ISBN: 978-0-9829404-1-9

All rights reserved. No portion of this book may be copied, reproduced or transmitted in any form without prior written permission from the publisher.

Printed in the United States of America

Social Inspiration Aric J. Henderson

Foreword

I first met Aric during his freshmen year of college. At the invitation of friends and former high school classmates, Aric was invited to worship with us at the Christian Campus House. As I recall, he came only once as a visitor and after that, many times as family, inviting other hungry beggars to a banquet set by the bread of life. I soon discovered that this magnetic and charismatic young man was passionate about two things—maybe three if we count food—people and Jesus. Mizzou's own "Social Network," Aric was engaged in multiple, overlapping circles of campus and community circles, not because he craved attention, but, because Christ in him compelled others.

Social Inspiration is the powerful reflection of a man who has seen enough of the world to know that he was created for another; yet, is not content to arrive there alone. Out of the overflow of a heart that has been in the valley and on the mountaintop, Aric speaks. He is keenly aware of how God puts people and objects in his path to bless him as well as to cause him to be a blessing. Listen, and you will hear the voice of God as He meditates through the mind of Aric.

Lance Tamerius, Director
Christian Campus House
University of Missouri - Columbia

Social Inspiration   Aric J. Henderson

Social Inspiration   Aric J. Henderson

TABLE OF CONTENTS

Introduction   vi

A Word from the Author   vii

School Life Before College   viii

Aric's College Experience   ix

Quotes   2-32

Introduction

It is not uncommon for a young Christian to go off to college and "forget" everything they learned in church and do the opposite of what their parents taught them throughout their life. They often begin doing things such as going to parties, drinking, smoking and having sex.

Aric J. Henderson is a great example of a young man who remembered what had been instilled in him. During college, he attended church regularly and went on mission trips to Jamaica and Mississippi to help build a church, rebuild homes and deliver clothing. He also lived in the Christian Campus House. Even though he endured many worldly pressures, he associated himself with other Christians and remained strong in his faith throughout his college life.

This book is a manifestation of his dedication to represent Christ through his thoughts, words, and actions. You will be inspired as you read the words of wisdom found in *Social Inspiration* by Aric J. Henderson.

A Word From The Author

Ever since Middle school, I have always had a passion for words. I had a way of knowing what words meant when I or someone else said them. I did not have to look them up in the dictionary. Through reading my Bible and living a Christian life, I have learned that there is power in words. If you say something, it will come to pass.

One day, I had a conversation with an atheist about Jesus. He was well-educated and very knowledgeable about the words in the Bible. When I opened my mouth to try to witness to him, he told me that he could tell I was just repeating religious things I had heard from church. He told me that I did not have any real knowledge. So, I started studying words. But, most of all, I began studying my Bible more so I could gain a greater understanding.

I like to be original, so most of my quotes are my own original words. Writing positive things makes me a more effective witness to others.

Aric J. Henderson, Author
Social Inspiration

School Life Before College

In school, Aric was very social and had lots of friends. As a result, he was often reprimanded by his teachers for disrupting class and being "off task". It was in middle school where he began to redirect his social energy to more positive things. Aric had been sent to the principal's office on numerous occasions, due to unacceptable classroom behavior. One day, during his eighth grade year, he was sent to the office for being disruptive in class.

While reprimanding Aric, the assistant principal showed Aric a disciplinary folder which contained every behavior report he had received from sixth through eighth grade. Mr. Finger told Aric that with that number of behavior reports, he could have justifiably been suspended from school on several occasions. Furthermore, there was nothing to keep him from being suspended for the current infraction. But, Aric had never been suspended.

Seeing his large disciplinary file, Aric realized he had received a lot of undeserved chances; So, he made the decision, that day, to never misbehave in class again. That was his last visit to the office for behavior problems. By the time he got to high school, he was recognized as a student who had leadership ability and was often chosen to participate in special activities.

That office visit with Mr. Finger was the beginning of Aric taking responsibility for his actions; he also took responsibility for his future and began to prepare for college.

Social Inspiration Aric J. Henderson

Aric's College Experience

When Aric first went to college, his goal was to enter the journalism program. He had learned how to operate television cameras and had acted in numerous plays at church. He also took acting and journalism classes in high school.

But, by the end of his high school year, his grade point average was not high enough to immediately get accepted into the University of Missouri – Columbia's Journalism program. So, he began his freshman year of college working part-time at KOMU television news station. His goal was to gain the requirements for the journalism program by the end of his sophomore year so he could request admission to the School of Journalism.

At the end of his sophomore year, he was accepted into the School of Journalism. However, one day a speaker visited one of his journalism classes and spoke about the reality, including the good and the challenges, of working in the field of journalism. Aric listened intently as the speaker said "think about what you really enjoy doing". It was at that moment when Aric realized that what he really wanted to do was work in the area of sports; furthermore, he would be happy if he could be a football coach.

Realizing what he wanted to do as a career, he began to research the qualifications to become a football coach. Upon learning the qualifications, he changed his major to psychology and secured a student assistant position with the University of Missouri - Columbia's football team. He quit his part-time job to dedicate his time to learning all he could about becoming a football coach.

Social Inspiration   Aric J. Henderson

Aric graduated with his Bachelor's degree in December of 2010.

    It is uncertain where the road of life will take him. But, one thing is for certain, Aric's faith will keep him lined up with God's perfect will.

Social Inspiration

Aric J. Henderson

Imagine our United States president going to Iraq, grabbing his gun and bullet proof vest and fighting on the front lines to save America. Sounds silly huh? The most powerful man in the country laying down his life for his people...But wait! The *King of the universe* already did that. Now tell me *that* King doesn't deserve my allegiance.

****

I don't want to just be good, I want excellence. I want to be the *best*! But the best only get to be that by *outworking* everyone... that part scares me.

****

Sometimes it is good to look back and remember what we used to be and what we used to get into and see how the Holy Spirit has changed us. We should not beat ourselves up so much; Jesus already took that punishment! We are able to walk in freedom and righteousness because of His grace! I am not all that I want to be, but I am surely not what I used to be! I am *changed*.

****

I am *dying* to see my Lord's face! This world offers me absolutely *nothing* of value outside of my redemption. I want it in the worse way!

****

Contentness (it's not a real word, but, back off, it's my quote) is sooooo weird. I haven't been here very often. I don't know what to do with myself.

Social Inspiration

Aric J. Henderson

I boast in this cross and nothing else! I'm kind of lame without it.

****

Let me just be in the background for a little while. God, You be the face and let me just sit and glean from You. Like Peter, I know I can be a knuckle head, but, I'm chasing Your heart with relentless pursuit.

****

Suitcase in hand and door locked behind me. Nothing to the left. Nothing to the right. But, I look skyward and keep moving.

****

Back to the basics. Me and *You*. Feels good!

****

To be where You are is my heart's desire.

****

Some people call it growth... I say it feels like mayhem.

****

Hey, see the real big dude holding the universe? Yeah, He's on my team. *Next*!

****

Jesus makes everything beautiful! Wow!

Social Inspiration   Aric J. Henderson

Dear Money, I've made it without much of you before. You come and go. Dear nice car, you move on the road just like my car, only difference is you cost more to fix. Dear Alcohol, I have so much joy and it is no thanks to you. Dear women, my heart was spoken for 2000 years ago... sorry.

****

Who wants to change the world with me?

****

I didn't decide to follow Jesus because I was a great person. I don't know where you got that idea from. I follow Jesus because I'm broken. I follow Jesus because I have nothing to offer anyone. I follow Jesus because I remember the days when I had no friends. I follow Jesus because He took me the way I was and still am... worthless.

****

There is no treasure greater than my Daddy's heart. No love realer. Nothing more satisfying and nothing more consistent. Real love does exist. It died and rose before I was even born! This is true beauty!

****

My deceitful heart has tricked me for the last time. Jesus I'm after your heart cause mine keeps letting me down.

****

Social Inspiration

Aric J. Henderson

Please don't let me miss the little things that make life so spectacular! Busyness without heavenly purpose is a waste of a life.

****

Without Him, I am drained. With Him, I am refreshed!

****

How could I let true love slip through my fingers? This world has nothing for me! One false move and I'm face to face with my maker, one slip up and all friends are gone. There's one true love, one passion, one forgiveness, and one that I answer to. Fill my cup and let it overflow.

****

There is nothing greater than the love that holds my life in His hands.

****

Focus...

****

One day you are on top and the next, you're crashed on the shores of the beaches of life. But one thing never changes... My God's passion for His creation. Let my heart be ever chasing that love!

****

Crumble my perception of truth and mold me to Your heart's desire.

Social Inspiration

Aric J. Henderson

Separation…. my burden, darkness, anger, confusion…. three *Nails*, pain, tears, death, conquest, freedom, light, righteousness, running, hope, *Love*! That's a *beautiful exchange*!

****

Oh how I desire the faith of an uninhibited child! Trusting, wishful, hopeful, caring, and free of embarrassment as they run around and play made up games with their imaginary friends in the yard. No chains, no barriers, no distractions. Lord, give me that.

****

God's love is strong! Can you hear the Father's heart?

****

When I don't know what to do, I just stand.

****

I am thankful for my good friends who are always encouraging, praying for, and uplifting me. I need it too sometimes.

****

There is redemption all around! It's in everything, it's all around. Creation screams it.

****

I'm trying to be like David; I'm gunning for Your heart Jesus.

Social Inspiration

Aric J. Henderson

You are my delight and my reward.

****

I have one purpose, and like Albert Pujols said, "it satisfies my soul forever."

****

Today, we answer the call of greatness... the moment is now!

****

Let the earth shake before our Holy God! Let man bow before His throne.

****

Praise the Lord of creation who is coming back. With child-like faith we will wait on him!

****

Sense the *power* of His ever beckoning love!

****

My heart was deceived. I thought I knew what love was. Then You gave my heart a new song and taught me how to *love*! Now You have me open like the book of Psalms and I want more!

****

My sin is great before a *Holy* God!

Social Inspiration Aric J. Henderson

Creation is pointing to God's glory and its beauty worships Him night and day!

****

I don't need to be in a relationship, I need my God to save me from this flesh and a perfect love that purifies and makes me righteous.

****

I have learned that thought becomes word, word becomes action, action becomes habit, and habit becomes character.

****

Dear Jesus, I want to give You everything, but, all I have is this brokenness and sin to offer and yet You still offer me joy, peace and wisdom. My cost doesn't seem to match the bill.

****

It's like I've read this chapter before; just different characters.

****

Keeping my hands in the hands of the only hands I trust.

****

This is true love and I'm immersed in it! Lord, never cease to let the little things about Your character amaze me.

****

Social Inspiration — Aric J. Henderson

Wow, so this is what contentment feels like? Just enjoying life huh? I'm just so used to worrying about the future I never actually realized I could enjoy the day in front of me, I think I'll try this trusting God thing more often.

****

I will wait for You Lord because Your timing is perfect.

****

I guess the grind is never over. There is always something to accomplish; always something you can do better; and always a hater or two to keep you inspired.

****

I thank God for my mother, who always has my back.

****

I come undone before a perfect King!

****

His pull is strengthening.

****

I don't have the heart or means to pay the asking price... Jesus, thank you!

****

I got You, I got everything!

Social Inspiration   Aric J. Henderson

My King does not share his throne. It fits *one* and that's the one who gave it all. Tell me how Zeus changed your life and redeemed you?

****

I'll never forget the day I was drug out of death. Jesus, You'll always be the love of my life.

****

Face to the ground, heart to the sky. Lord, fill me up.

****

Lord, let me be in awe of the little things every day.

****

On this day, my day of birth let the LORD be glorified!

****

Those who wait on the Lord renew their strength. Timeless Bible verse!

****

I was trippin' then Jesus said "Yo Aric?" I was like "huh?" and he was like "My yoke is easy and my burden is light." Then I was like "Oh yeah!" Now I'm gravy.

****

There is nothing more beautiful than two children of God coming together under His sovereignty in marriage.

Social Inspiration

Aric J. Henderson

Lord, I'm still a little child in need of a father.

****

I am broken without You! I'll look to You.

****

Take heart! The God who holds the *universe* in his *hand* is in control. What better situation to have than the God of all days running the show?

****

One purpose, Jesus. One way, Jesus. One motivation, Jesus. One reason to breathe, ...I'm sure you can guess where I'm going with this. In case you don't know though, it's *Jesus*.

****

I need Jesus like the power rangers need to morph, like pancakes need peanut butter!

****

It's becoming more and more apparent that men of God don't know how to talk to women. Say what you mean and mean what you say. We let our mouths write checks our hearts can't cash.

****

I was just the kid getting in trouble everyday for trying to make everybody laugh. I wasn't supposed to be here. The cross is MIGHTY!

Social Inspiration Aric J. Henderson

For the broken hearted and abandoned; the outcast and fatherless; for the forgotten and lost and those who love like there's no tomorrow, but, who are not loved back, my heart breaks for you! Keep pushing... help is on the way. Our God reigns and He sits on a throne of limitless LOVE!

****

Just give me one day in Your presence. Just one.

****

So wait... I don't get heaven points every time I do something good? You mean I could never possibly earn my way to heaven even if I tried with all my heart? You're telling me Jesus will take me as I am and do the work in me? *No.* That's like telling me I never had anything to offer to the Lord except a broken and obedient heart.

****

If you have been an underdog your whole life, don't stop grinding! We push because nobody is going to give us anything. Don't forget *your* story! Don't forget where you started off. Don't forget the pain. Don't forget the doubters and haters... and don't forget the ones that didn't want you. God opens doors *no man* can shut. This cross is *all* we got!

****

In every season I have a reason to worship. Whether I'm in the desert or in abundance, I got to go hard for my King!

Social Inspiration

Aric J. Henderson

If April showers bring May flowers, we are about to get like fifty billion flowers!

****

All I want to hear is Your voice! All my eyes want to see is Your glory.

****

I wish my words could express what's in my heart.

****

How can I describe an event that took place... 15,000 believers worshiping the ONE true God. The God that called me out of my destructive life. The God that took me as I was! The God who cleaned me up. The worship doesn't stay in one place. Oh no! I'm taking it with me *everywhere*!

****

God you are my EVERYTHING! Consume me and be glorified in this nothingness that is Aric Henderson.

****

This goes out to the men who know how to treat a woman. You guard her heart. You don't push her into anything she does not want. She is better just for having been around you. You pray for her. You pray *with* her. You are patient with her and want the absolute best for her. You want to meet all the people that mean the most to her. You don't abuse her with your words; and you wouldn't *dare* abuse her physically. You my friend, are a real man.

Social Inspiration   Aric J. Henderson

Lord, let my breath be for Your love. Let my walk be for Your glory. Let my talk be for the advancement of Your Word.

****

I want You in the worst way, Lord. I have got to have You! I can't breathe without You. I can't even *think* about my next step without You guiding it. Have Your way.

****

I am focused on *two* things: pleasing my Lord and being the greatest at what I do. Period.

****

There is a love I have come to know; a love that fulfills every promise; a love that consumes my soul; a love whose heart breaks every time my heart breaks; a love that finishes what it starts and breathes life into me every day. There is a love I have come to know; that satisfies my every desire and every longing. Can I tell you about it?

****

I walk fast because every step has a purpose. I walk slow so I don't miss *a thing*.

****

My God is so beautiful. Thank You, Lord for the little things.

****

Social Inspiration   Aric J. Henderson

Dear Jamaica, I can't shake you. I miss the smell of your mountain rain. Your streets of red dirt. The way you put jerk seasoning on *everything*! The way you served me fresh coconuts and neasberries from your tree tops. Your beautiful accent. And of course Ding Dong. Duh. I will be back soon, have no worries. Love, an insignificant American

****

The Lord is magnificent in His splendor and in all of His ways.

****

My heart still yearns for those mountains of brokenness. On that hill my Father showed the extent of His love for a fallen creation.

****

My King sits on the throne of love.

****

I get my hands dirty because I *have* to. Nobody is going to give me anything.

****

I am a winner and second place is not acceptable. My Daddy sits over all creation like a boss. I guess you haven't heard... it's in the blood.

****

Social Inspiration   Aric J. Henderson

Well, the Lord said, "don't be anxious for anything." So I guess that's my cue to *quit worrying* about stuff. It's in Your hands now Lord. I am going to go enjoy this day ...or maybe this *life*.

****

I got that new iGrind. It is a drive that only comes from *my* supplier. And he has supplied the nations since the beginning of time. Same thing, different name.

****

I wish I could bottle up true beauty.

****

Compassion is a *beautiful* thing!

****

It seems like for years I have tried to be perfect, like I ever had that power anyway. But, now I just want to be who Jesus says I am...Redeemed by Grace.

****

I serve an audience of one, but, I stand watched by many.

****

I do things *one* way: all out. I got *one* speed: full. There is *one* way to the top: through my Lord.

****

Social Inspiration

Aric J. Henderson

Give me lemons and I will make lemonade with some lemon-squeezed chicken and mashed potatoes; and for dessert I will make some lemon pie with lemon ice cream on top! Hungry? I am.

****

When His blood poured out! When He carried that cross! When He let *a man*! that *He* created whip His back! *His* back! I was purchased! My life is *brand new*! Do *you* hear me? Brand new! Get to know Him please!
His love is insurmountable!

****

God, hear my heart! My desire is to be consumed! No imitations. No fakes. Not my idols, but, Your heart!

****

I have seen the face of Love. They still haven't created an English word that can embody the vision of true love. Maybe I should learn Russian or something; they might have a word for it.

****

My heart leaps into my throat and my stomach turns in anticipation of a love truer than what I have been offered so far.

****

Grace, please come to my rescue. Save me from my heart of pride. Sometimes I doubt You. But I know I need You.

Social Inspiration   Aric J. Henderson

I am *nothing*, not anything, zero, without my Love, my Friend, my King, my Advisor, my Father, my Heartbeat.

****

I couldn't imagine living for anything else besides the love that completes my soul!

****

Every beat of my heart is for the passion poured out for me on that hill! I breathe grace with every inhale. I run full speed to love; and if you get in my way....

****

I can smell the desperation in the air. One more night and you might see the sunlight; and if you climb out of bed there is a world waiting to destroy you. So, I grind for all those forgotten.

****

The Bible says, "Man makes plans; God orders his steps"... So, I'll keep marching.

****

Time to punch in on the clock. There's work to do and you know I'm about my Father's business!

****

Although I turned my back on Him countless times; Being one of the crowd mocking him; one of the soldiers ripping His back to shreds; one of the Pharisees rejecting His every word as he poured out His life line that was His blood; He still looked me in the eyes and said, "My *desire* is to be gracious to you." Isaiah 30:18.

****

I had a drink this morning. It opened my eyes. I was so *satisfied*. It was so *quenching*. I would even say this drink changed my life. It came from a spring that never ceases to flow and a river that is clear as crystal. I can't stop drinking it. I need more of it. This *water* lives in my veins. This *water* is my source of living... I guess that's why they call Him the Living Water.

****

I will follow Jesus wherever he goes. I answer to one man! My Lord.

****

God, thank you for the little things that mean so much! You truly are a gentleman.

****

Hold on. He's all you got right now.

****

You just do things differently when you realize you belong to the King of the universe.

****

Either sin must die or I will. The self must be denied so that it won't be destroyed.

Social Inspiration

Aric J. Henderson

Call me a glow stick cause I glow in the dark. Call me a camp fire cause I'm about to light up the night.

****

I'm not a Christian because I never mistakes, I'm a Christian because I *always* make mistakes. Where would I be without grace!

****

I never really had anything in this world but a Savior that loved me with all His heart; and that, my friend, is truth!

****

I know I got the "real deal" because my joy never fades! So that's why I'm never satisfied. I knew that water tasted funny. No more sewer water for me. Only living water for now on!

****

Then my Lord looked me in the eyes and said "You ready?" I said nothing. He began to walk away. Then the thought of a life without him gripped my heart and I grabbed my cross and followed him... never to look back.

****

It's the little things that matter. All it takes is a smile to transform someone else's day.

****

Social Inspiration

Aric J. Henderson

It's not about me and never was. I'll be dead in about 40 years - God willing - and the world won't even remember my name. But, Lord, I pray my love would be my legacy.

****

You only live once. So I say, *why not*! I'm not sure if life could be any better than this! Lord, you complete me!

****

All I ever wanted was true love. All my heart ever longed for was a love that accepted me for who I was. All I ever wanted was for someone to care about me the same way I cared about them. I looked high, I looked low and when I was weary and tired my Love found me. My Love put my weary heart to rest. My Love wanted me.

****

I told the Love of my life I want to go to the next level. All of a sudden I couldn't breathe. I asked my Savior what was happening, He said "at this level the only air you have is me. Anything that is not me will suffocate you. For now on, I am the air you breathe."

****

Holy are You, Lord! There were none before You and there will be none after You! You are *my King*!

****

I am someone because I love You.

****

Social Inspiration — Aric J. Henderson

I never really was that good of a guy, huh? Even in His weakest state, my King was the only thing righteous about me.

****

There is no one else for me! I have one goal in this life, and that is to bring my Father praise. With every breath I inhale! With every thought that passes through my mind. With every step I take let my Father who is in heaven be pleased by His servant.

****

So, this is what it feels like to just live. I have to try this no worrying thing more often.

****

No need to rush, enjoy the little things sometimes.

****

Sometimes having too much too soon will make you weak. Strength is what you do with what life gives you.

****

Excuses are not an option, only opportunity lies ahead.

****

Your will is what I desire; not my own.

****

Social Inspiration

Aric J. Henderson

I got t-shirts and underwear for Christmas and it's probably the best one I've ever had! I love my family! My mom is so wise! She's always looking out for me and she always has my back! If I had to go to war with one person it just might be her.

****

I wouldn't be anywhere without you, Mom! Your advice always rings in my head and you never mislead me. Thank you. I love you more than you know!

****

Living in the moment is not always the best idea but *now* is all we have! Yesterday is dead and tomorrow is not promised. I was created for this moment.

****

I was created for greatness, I promise I won't let anything get in my way.

****

Trying to please others is draining! My life is about to get a lot easier. Because from now on, I only have one constituent to please. Check please!

****

I can't imagine a love any greater. It doesn't exist! A heart so tender has never been and will never be. You carry my cross, let me never forget.

****

Social Inspiration   Aric J. Henderson

My God, You satisfy me! *You* hold my heart! *I love it*!

****

Sometimes you have to make it happen; not waiting on no one for *nothing*.

****

Thank you, haters, for lighting my fire. Now you are going to need more than that weak water hose to put me out.

****

It's the beauty in tragedy that saved my life. I won't look back!

****

The arithmetic of my life is this cross; I was lost in discovery and found in the simple complexity of His Love.

****

I can finally exhale! But, know that while you are sleeping I'm still in preparation.

****

Work hard to get on top, work harder to stay on top!

****

What's life without a couple of risks.

****

Social Inspiration

Aric J. Henderson

And when there's nothing else to say, and nowhere else to go, be still and know the King of the universe is working things out for you!

****

Why worry? All we can do is what's in front of us, so do that with excellence then move to the next task.

****

Could my heart attest to a love any greater than the love poured out for me on that cross? I can't even fathom it!

****

I bleed desire and success is my only option!

****

The beauty of hindsight lies in its clarity.

****

I don't *ever* want to get used to the message of the cross! Can we fall in love every day, Lord?

****

I tried to understand why He does what He does and still I don't know. There's nothing in this relationship for Him and *everything* in it for me. I get all the benefits and He takes all my shame, pain and guilt. Seems lop-sided. Lord, I promise I'm going to do better!

****

Social Inspiration   Aric J. Henderson

I'm learning to just live life with a smile. It's too short, you only get one. Enjoy the simple things; there's enough complexity in the world. Why make it more difficult?

****

Embrace the people God has put in your life! Don't push good friends away because of your pride.

****

Some people do. Some people say. All I know is God opens doors *no man* can shut.

****

Now is the time to relish the moment. A wise man once said, "be as gentle as a dove and as wise as a serpent".

****

You know that feeling you get when you know you screwed up something good. Yeah...

****

You had me on the ropes taking your best shots, then you looked in my eyes and realized you were in the fight of your life. What you failed to realize was that I have a guy in my corner that has never lost a fight.

****

I don't care what you look like; just have a heart like Jesus and care about me. Hurt when I hurt. Smile when I smile and I promise I'll give you the world!

Social Inspiration
Aric J. Henderson

I want to see the depths of Your majesty.

****

My feet were running so fast to the middle of nowhere; I guess I wasn't really running anywhere, because when I looked around I was in the same place I started. Big Man placed me heavenward now I am sprinting full speed. Only difference is the purpose that I take each step with.

****

You can call me brain washed; I just say I'm stained washed.

****

There is a love that I long for; worshiping You Jesus is what my heart desires. To return to my Creator is my passion.

****

Ok Love, I surrender.

****

I spent years chasing respect; it let me down. Then I tried women; even bigger let down. Next up was money; never could keep it. Material? Someone's always got better. Then I chased *You* and my life has never been the same! Thank You, Jesus. How could I ever repay You? All I have is this filthy heart.

****

Social Inspiration

Aric J. Henderson

My passion is this cross! They say I act brand new, but you would too if you knew what I had! Love that lasts until this earth disintegrates and even then, I'm still loved!

****

I am not what I want to be, but, not who I used to be. Praise the Creator of my soul for that!

****

If my life is an open book you must be reading the chapter on resilience.

****

I'm tired of this, but, if I am not dead I can only get stronger. Call this my cardio builder because the stamina is strong.

****

I stand all poured out; Lord, fill me with Your never ending joy; that carries me thru the valley of death; that seeks to consume my soul. God, I crave You!

****

Then I get a reminder; this is why I do this.

****

Smalls minds stay in small places. The world is bigger than *you*! You think everyone else's life revolves around yours, but, one day no one will even remember your

Social Inspiration   Aric J. Henderson

name and only the name of Jesus will remain. Lord I anticipate *that* day with great anxiousness!

****

Call this my dissertation. God is good, therefore life is good.

****

You spend money to look like you have money and the result is, you have no money. Irony...

****

I'm on that cross game.

****

I now see what I was so blind to; the pain makes you better. If you are grinding or hurting, fight for tomorrow. Joy is coming. Promise.

****

My King overcomes fear! Count one for the good guys!

****

A couple tears run but one can only hope to see me give up!

****

This is the final blow, the one of victory, to the chest then I hit him low. I had my wind knocked out of me - *gasp*! - But, I don't die!

Social Inspiration — Aric J. Henderson

Got a mean one at my back, I call it the cross. You can call Him the boss. Without my Daddy, I'm so lost! My first love and my last, now I take my seat. I'm ready for class. Teach me, Lord.

****

I am under the dirt, a man of low position. Feeling like my soul's passion is separated from my heart's desire. Give me revelation of Your glory, Lord.

****

My stomach stays growling because I'm so hungry! I'm not full yet so I keep stuffing my face. I'm going to clean my plate and everybody else's, too. You can call me a glutton on this one. I want this or the grave! No other option!

****

I don't want to be on the surface anymore! God, hear me out. I ask you, with my full heart, please take me deeper.

****

Who would've thought that day would change my entire existence, my entire purpose, my internal desire. Why You chose me, I'll never know.

****

I'm the skinny kid with glasses from 80th and Wayne. I'm not supposed to be here.

****

Social Inspiration   Aric J. Henderson

Your swag is manufactured, straight from the factory. My swag is genetic; let's just say I get it from my Daddy.

****

Call this my funeral, one of the voluntary type. I have lived for myself and I went nowhere faster than anyone.

****

Now comes the painful part... accepting love I don't deserve.

****

If the Lord tells the wind to go east, does it not go east? ...and if He says let there be light, is there not light? Then why do I worry about such little things that are not under my control? I'll be in the passenger seat chillin', I'm tired of driving.

****

I gotta fight for my life *every day*. The only easy day was yesterday.

****

Would you go to the hospital or the emergency room because you were healthy? Then why would you try to "get right" to come to Jesus. I'm in the hospital and I'm sharing a room with an alcoholic. Next door is a homosexual and a guy from my church who tells lies. There's no level of sin. It all separates us from Christ. Jesus said, "come as you are". I can't figure out why the world is fighting Jesus' words.

Social Inspiration

Aric J. Henderson

I am dirt. One day I'll be the good guy everyone thinks I am...

****

They won't give you anything... Every penny must be earned. Every opportunity must be *taken*. Every ounce of respect must be fought for. Nothing will "just happen", you have to *make it happen*. You can't just want it; everyone else wants it, too. At some point, something has to set you apart...*drive*.

****

Social Inspiration　　　　　　　Aric J. Henderson

Books and Resources published by Inspirations by Grace LaJoy

A Gifted Child in Foster Care: *A Story of Resilience*
(Book, Teacher's Guide, Student Workbook)

Writer's Breakthrough:
Steps To Copyright and Publish Your Own Book
(Book and CD)

More Than Mere Words: *Poetry That Ministers*
(Christian Poetry Book)

Poetic Empowerment
(Spoken Word CD)

Poetic Book Series
Diversity in our Schools, Diversity in our Workplace
The Bad Butt Kids, He's Worth It, Our Employees…Our Cornerstones

Sexual Purity and the Young Woman:
A Guide to Sexual Purity (Book)

My Automobile Dealership
(Book)

Diversity and My Credit Union
(Book)

To learn more please visit us online at
www.gracelajoy.com

www.ingramcontent.com/pod-product-compliance
Lightning Source LLC
Chambersburg PA
CBHW050608300426
44112CB00013B/2129